Woodland SDA School
128 E. Barnhart Rd.
Coldwater, MI 49036

NATURE'S MONSTERS

LIZARDS

Brenda Ralph Lewis

Please visit our web site at: **www.garethstevens.com**
For a free color catalog describing Gareth Stevens Publishing's
list of high-quality books and multimedia programs,
call 1-800-542-2595 (USA) or 1-800-387-3178 (Canada).
Gareth Stevens Publishing's fax: (414) 332-3567.

Library of Congress Cataloging-in-Publication Data

Lewis, Brenda Ralph.
    Lizards / Brenda Ralph Lewis. — North American ed.
       p. cm. — (Nature's monsters: Reptiles & amphibians)
    Includes bibliographical references and index.
    ISBN 0-8368-6173-6 (lib. bdg.)
    1. Lizards—Juvenile literature. I. Title. II. Series.
 QL666.L2L46   2006
 597.9—dc22   2005054175

This North American edition first published in 2006 by
Gareth Stevens Publishing
A Member of the WRC Media Family of Companies
330 West Olive Street, Suite 100
Milwaukee, WI 53212 USA

Original edition and illustrations copyright © 2006 by International Masters Publishers AB.
Produced by Amber Books Ltd., Bradley's Close, 74–77 White Lion Street, London N1 9PF, U.K.

Project editor: Michael Spilling
Design: Joe Conneally

Gareth Stevens editorial direction: Valerie J. Weber
Gareth Stevens art direction: Tammy West
Gareth Stevens production: Jessica Morris

All rights reserved. No part of this book may be reproduced, stored in a retrieval system,
or transmitted in any form or by any means, electronic, mechanical, photocopying, recording,
or otherwise, without the prior written permission of the copyright holder.

Printed in the United States of America

1 2 3 4 5 6 7 8 9 10 09 08 07 06

Contents

Basilisk Lizard	4
Ground Chameleon Lizard	6
Jackson's Chameleon	8
Panther Chameleon	10
Frilled Lizard	12
Flying Lizard	14
Gila Monster	16
Green Iguana	18
Regal Horned Lizard	20
Leaf-Tailed Gecko	22
Nile Monitor	24
Salvadori's Monitor	26
Bearded Dragon	28
Glossary	30
For More Information	31
Index	32

Continents of the World

The world is divided into seven continents — North America, South America, Europe, Africa, Asia, Australasia, and Antarctica. In this book, the area where each animal lives is shown in red, while all land is shown in green.

Words that appear in the glossary are printed in **boldface** type the first time they occur in the text.

Basilisk Lizard

The basilisk (BA-suh-lisk) **lizard**'s brown or green skin helps **camouflage** its body in bushes and other plants.

A basilisk lizard's long, thin tail keeps it upright when it is running.

The lizard can run at high speeds because of its strong, powerful legs.

Long fingers and sharp claws give the basilisk lizard a strong grip for climbing trees.

Basilisk lizards are also called "Jesus Christ" lizards. The Bible tells of Christ walking on water. Basilisk lizards can do that, too, because of the shape of their back feet.

Size

Did You Know?

There is a difference between the male and the female basilisk lizard. Only the male has a **crest** of skin that runs all the way from its head to its tail.

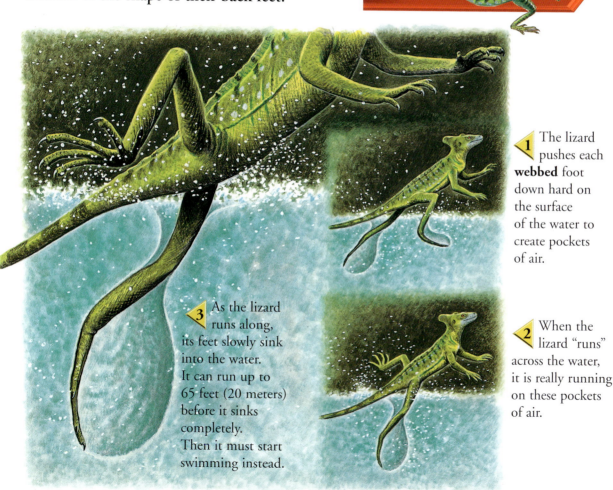

1 The lizard pushes each **webbed** foot down hard on the surface of the water to create pockets of air.

2 When the lizard "runs" across the water, it is really running on these pockets of air.

3 As the lizard runs along, its feet slowly sink into the water. It can run up to 65 feet (20 meters) before it sinks completely. Then it must start swimming instead.

Where in the World

Basilisk lizards live near rivers and streams in the thick forests of Central America and northern South America. They grow from 24 to 30 inches (61 to 76 centimeters) in length.

Ground Chameleon Lizard

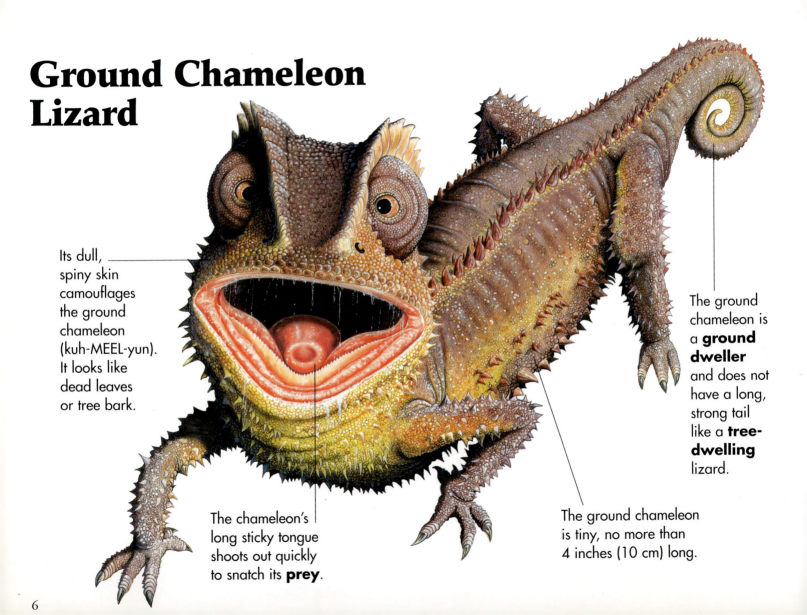

Its dull, spiny skin camouflages the ground chameleon (kuh-MEEL-yun). It looks like dead leaves or tree bark.

The chameleon's long sticky tongue shoots out quickly to snatch its **prey**.

The ground chameleon is a **ground dweller** and does not have a long, strong tail like a **tree-dwelling** lizard.

The ground chameleon is tiny, no more than 4 inches (10 cm) long.

Male chameleons will often fight over food and **territory**. When two **rival** male chameleons fight, the battle can be fierce and deadly.

1 Each of these chameleons wants to drive his rival away. They start by staring each other in the eye, opening their mouths wide, and making angry side-to-side movements.

2 Neither chameleon is willing to move away, so they must fight. They fling themselves at each other, biting with their strong jaws and gripping with their thin but strong legs. The battle lasts until one of the lizards is too badly injured to continue.

Actual Size

Did You Know?

Ground chameleons can remain completely still for hours on end. Sometimes they keep still to protect themselves from **predators**. At other times, they wait for the insects they eat to pass by.

Where in the World

There are about twenty-four species of ground chameleons. Most live on the island of Madagascar off the eastern coast of Africa. Others live in the **savannas** and **tropical** forests of Central Africa.

Jackson's Chameleon

Both male and female Jackson's chameleons have three horns on their heads.

The chameleon's tongue is 12 inches (30 cm) long — almost as long as the chameleon itself.

Nose to tail, Jackson's chameleon measures up to 12.5 inches (32 cm) long.

When hunting, the chameleon's eyes move forward to **focus** on its prey.

The Jackson's chameleon can judge the exact distance it must cover to grab the insects it eats as food. Then, it uses its long, muscled tongue to attack.

1 When it is not using it for hunting, the Jackson's chameleon's long tongue lies wrinkled up in its mouth.

2 When the chameleon is close enough to its prey, the sticky pad at the end of its tongue starts to hang out of its mouth. Moments later, the chameleon shoots out its tongue with great speed.

3 In only one-fourth of a second, the Jackson's chameleon has caught the prey with the end of its tongue and pulled it back into its mouth.

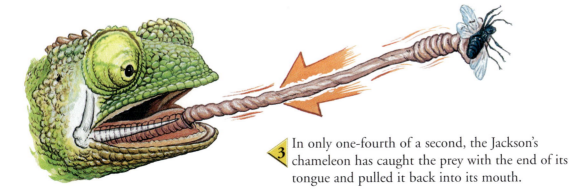

Size

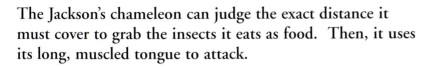

Did You Know?

Jackson's chameleons warm their blood by sitting in the sun. Dark skin warms up more quickly than pale skin, so the chameleons turn their skin darker before they start "sunbathing."

Where in the World

The Jackson's chameleon lives in the trees and bushes in the **highlands** of eastern Africa, close to Mount Kenya and the Aberdare Mountains in Kenya and Mount Usambara in Tanzania.

Panther Chameleon

The **chromatophores** in its skin enable the chameleon to change color.

The panther chameleon opens its mouth wide to eat insects and frighten rivals.

The panther chameleon can hang from tree branches using its strong, **flexible** tail.

Its curved toes allow the chameleon to grip the branches of trees very firmly.

The panther chameleon can be a fierce fighter. It has one unusual weapon — when it becomes really angry, it can change its colors as a warning to rivals and enemies.

Size

Did You Know?

On Madagascar, many people fear panther chameleons because of their fierce, colorful appearance. Cars and other traffic stop when a pantheon chameleon crosses the road.

1 A panther chameleon walking along a small branch comes face to face with a rival. The panther chameleon is determined to get rid of its smaller rival. As it grows more and more pushy, the chromatophores in its skin make its colors much brighter.

Where in the World

Most panther chameleons **inhabit rain forests** on the island of Madagascar off the eastern coast of Africa. They can also be found on other islands in the Indian Ocean, such as Nosi Bé, Réunion, and Mauritius.

2 The colors of the larger panther chameleon change from dull green to dangerous-looking red and orange. The skin color of its much smaller rival gets paler and paler. At last, the rival decides to leave; it crawls away, defeated.

Frilled Lizard

The frill surrounds the frilled lizard's head except at the back of its neck.

With its mouth open, the lizard looks frightening, but it does not harm humans.

The frilled lizard has scales all over its body, like protective armor.

Wherever the frilled lizard lives, its skin color blends in with its surroundings.

Frilled lizards try to **bluff** their enemies away. These tricks, however, do not always work, so sometimes the lizard has to try something else.

Size

Did You Know?

Together with the kangaroo, the frilled lizard is one of the symbols of Australia. This dramatic-looking **reptile** has appeared on the Australian two-cent coin and on the country's postage stamps.

1 The frilled lizard is in danger. The first thing it does is keep still, hoping that its color will hide it from its enemy.

3 The lizard's enemy is not frightened away, so the lizard stands up on its back legs and waves its claws, jaws, and tail. If its enemy still is not frightened, the frilled lizard will give up and run away.

Where in the World

The frilled lizard lives in the tropical regions of northern Australia and southern Papua New Guinea.

2 This trick does not work, so the lizard becomes threatening. It opens its mouth wide and uses two rods made of bone to spread out its big frill. It also hisses loudly.

Flying Lizard

It uses its long tail to help it change direction while gliding.

The flying lizard **glides** by spreading out flaps of skinlike wings.

The lizard's spotted skin allows it to hide when lying on tree trunks.

The flying lizard uses its strong feet to climb trees in its rain forest **habitats**.

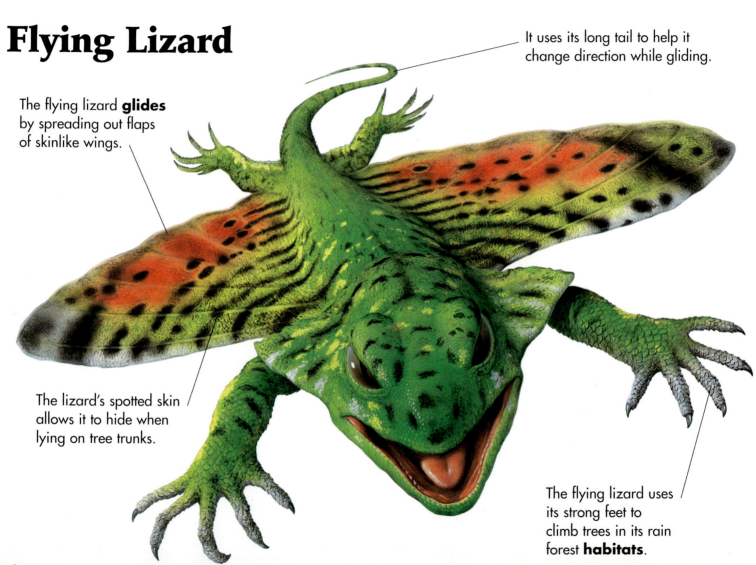

Flying lizards like to eat ants, termites, and other small insects, which they find on the trunks and branches of trees. They often surprise their prey with their ability to glide through the air.

1 The lizard sees a small beetle in a crack in the bark of a tree. Using its long tongue, it captures the beetle and eats it.

2 It is still hungry, so the lizard moves on to another tree nearby. It spreads its bright yellow "wings" and jumps into the air.

3 The lizard flattens its body and steers with its tail to land on the tree trunk. It starts climbing up, looking for more food.

Size

Did You Know?

Several other animals can also glide through the forest using flaps of skin. They include other lizards called geckos, squirrels, frogs, **marsupials**, and even a snake — the paradise tree snake.

Where in the World

Flying lizards live in the rain forests of Southeast Asia, including the Philippines, Malaysia, and Indonesia. They share these habitats with forty similar species of lizard.

Gila Monster

The gila monster delivers its **venom** through its lower teeth. The teeth each have two **grooves**.

The gila (HE-luh) monster has scales like beads that help it to blend into the desert landscape.

The gila monster stores fat from food in its tail to support it through the winter.

This lizard has short, powerful legs with big claws on its feet.

Gila monsters are the only poisonous lizards in North America. They use their teeth or their venom to **paralyze** or kill their prey. Gila monsters swallow their prey in one piece.

Size

Did You Know?

The gila monster goes hunting for food only in the spring and summer. When it has eaten enough, it spends the winter lying around in a sandy **burrow**.

1. This gila monster has followed a small snake by using its **forked tongue** to "taste" its scent in the air. When it reaches its prey, the gila opens its mouth wide.

2. The lizard pounces. It seizes the snake by the neck, sinks its teeth into its flesh, and pumps in its venom through its grooved lower teeth.

3. The little snake has no chance. Nothing can stop the gila monster from gulping it down head first. The snake vanishes inside the lizard.

Where in the World

Gila monsters are North American lizards. In the United States, they can be found in New Mexico, California, Nevada, Arizona, and Utah and also in the state of Sonora in northwestern Mexico.

Green Iguana

A mass of tiny scales covers the green iguana's (ih-GWAH-nuh) skin.

Green iguanas use scent **glands** under their thighs to mark their territory.

The reptile uses a flap of skin, or dewlap, under its throat to signal to other iguanas.

The iguana uses its long, sharp claws for climbing trees and digging.

Some people keep green iguanas as household pets, but they are not really tame like dogs, cats, or hamsters. Sometimes they still act like creatures living in the wild.

Size

Did You Know?

Green iguanas are often used to play dinosaurs in movies. In real life, they measure between 3 and 6 feet (0.9–1.8 meters), including the tail. Movie cameras make them look huge.

1. A pet male green iguana sits on a bookshelf in a room where his owner is watching television. For the iguana, this room is his territory, and his owner looks like a rival.

3. The iguana becomes angry and attacks his owner, who tries to protect himself. The iguana gives him several painful bites and scratches.

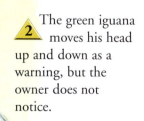

2. The green iguana moves his head up and down as a warning, but the owner does not notice.

Where in the World

Green iguanas live in central Mexico, Central America, and the northern part of South America. They also live on some Caribbean islands, such as Trinidad and Tobago.

Regal Horned Lizard

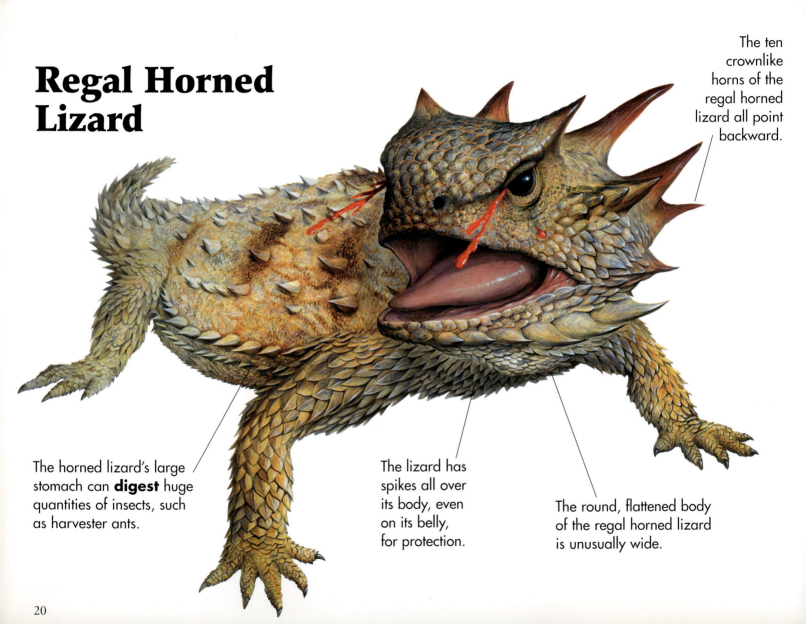

The ten crownlike horns of the regal horned lizard all point backward.

The horned lizard's large stomach can **digest** huge quantities of insects, such as harvester ants.

The lizard has spikes all over its body, even on its belly, for protection.

The round, flattened body of the regal horned lizard is unusually wide.

Regal horned lizards are often preyed upon by larger animals. Although their spiky appearance may put off some animals, their main defence is to squirt an irritating fluid at a predator.

Size

Did You Know?

This lizard can eat twenty–five hundred harvester ants in one meal. It is a slow eater and spends a long time in the intense heat of the desert while having its meals.

1. The regal horned lizard turns to face an approaching skunk. The lizard stays very stiff and still. It closes its eyes — but not out of fear. It is preparing a nasty surprise for the skunk.

2. The skunk is fooled into thinking that the lizard is not going to defend itself. Suddenly, from underneath its closed eyelids, the lizard shoots out jets of blood straight into the skunk's face. Shocked and startled, the skunk runs away.

Where in the World

The regal horned lizard lives in the harsh, rocky Sonoran desert that covers northwestern Mexico and the U.S. states of Arizona and New Mexico.

Leaf-Tailed Gecko

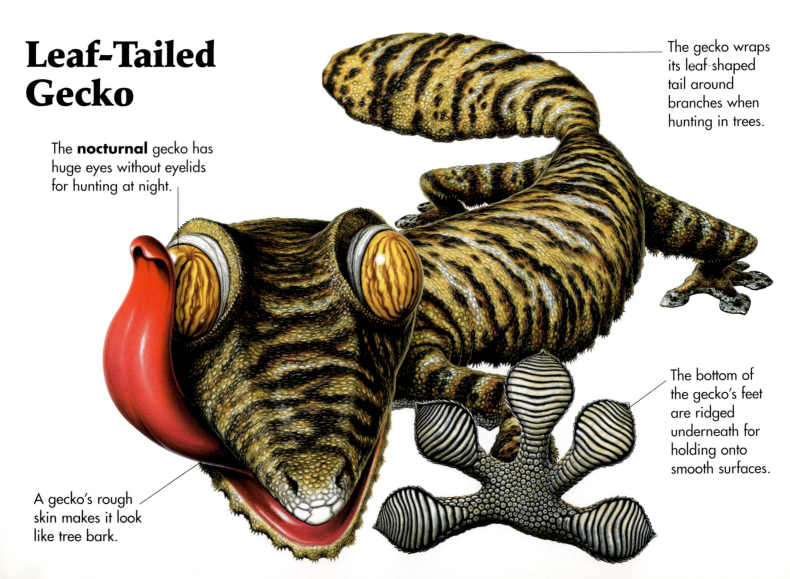

The **nocturnal** gecko has huge eyes without eyelids for hunting at night.

The gecko wraps its leaf-shaped tail around branches when hunting in trees.

A gecko's rough skin makes it look like tree bark.

The bottom of the gecko's feet are ridged underneath for holding onto smooth surfaces.

Small animals often hunt leaf-tailed geckos. Sometimes, the geckos will turn on their predators and hiss, hoping to frighten them away. At other times, they have to escape quickly to avoid being eaten.

1. The leaf-tailed gecko is suddenly disturbed by a wild cat that has climbed up the tree to eat the lizard. The gecko runs along the branch, and reaches the end.

2. The gecko jumps off the branch into the air. As it plunges downward, the gecko rolls itself up into a tight ball. It hits the ground, bounces twice but is not hurt.

3. Out of danger, the gecko unravels and heads for the nearest dense bushes and grass to hide from any other predators.

Size

Did You Know?

Because leaf-tailed geckos are active only after sunset, they cannot use the sun's heat to warm up. During the day, they sleep under tree bark to keep warm.

Where in the World

While other geckos live in every part of the world, leaf-tailed geckos can only be found on the island of Madagascar off the eastern coast of Africa.

Nile Monitor

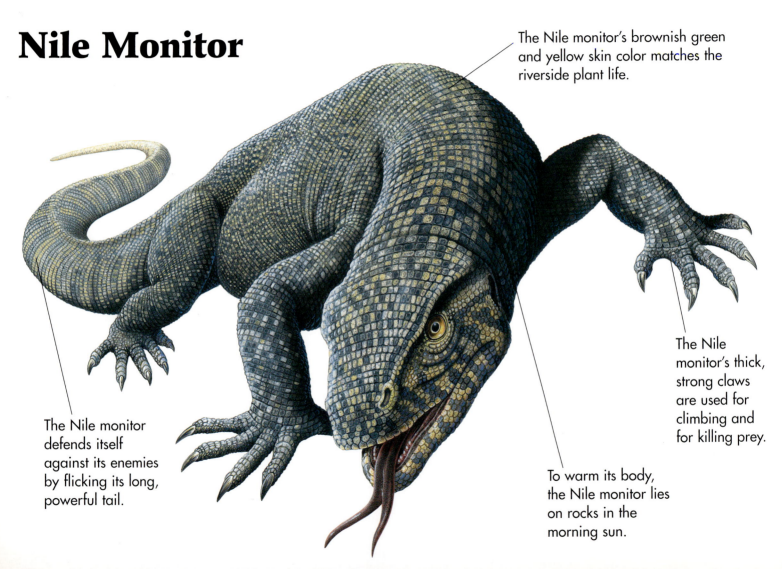

The Nile monitor's brownish green and yellow skin color matches the riverside plant life.

The Nile monitor's thick, strong claws are used for climbing and for killing prey.

To warm its body, the Nile monitor lies on rocks in the morning sun.

The Nile monitor defends itself against its enemies by flicking its long, powerful tail.

The Nile monitor will eat small animals, such as snails, crabs, snakes, frogs, and small lizards, and the eggs of other reptiles and birds.

Size

1. A mother crocodile buries her eggs for safety in the warm sand by a river. A **mongoose** starts sniffing around the eggs. The crocodile roars loudly and drives the mongoose away.

2. While the crocodile is busy scaring the mongoose, she does not notice the Nile monitor creeping toward the buried eggs. Before she can stop the monitor, it quickly digs down into the sand, then snatches an egg and runs off into a bush to eat it.

Did You Know?

Female Nile monitors can lay up to forty eggs at a time. Each weighs around 2 ounces (50 grams). The mother monitor grows to double her normal weight while carrying them.

Where in the World

Although Nile monitors are named after the Nile River in Egypt, they do not only live there. They also live near rivers in every part of Africa.

Salvadori's Monitor

The Salvadori's monitor's (SAL-vuh-DOOR-ees MAH-nuh-tur) tail is twice as long as its body and is used as a whip.

The Salvadori's monitor has extralong toes and sharp, curved claws for climbing trees.

It has teeth as sharp as razors and inflicts terrible bites.

As a male Salvadori's monitor ages, its **snout** becomes much wider.

Salvadori's monitor lizards have poor eyesight and sometimes panic when surprised away from their treetop habitat.

1. A tourist on vacation in New Guinea sees a Salvadori's monitor and decides to take a photograph.

2. As the tourist moves closer, the lizard becomes scared. It tries to run up the nearest tree to get away, but the tourist is the first upright shape it sees. Mistaking him for a tree, the monitor runs up the tourist instead! They are both very scared as they come face to face.

Size

Did You Know?

Salvadori's monitors spend most of their lives high up in the trees in the New Guinea rain forests. The first one was not discovered until 1878.

Where in the World

Salvadori's monitor lizards live in a very small area — in the tropical forests and **mangrove** swamps in southern New Guinea, an island in Southeast Asia.

Bearded Dragon

Extralarge scales around the lizard's eyes protect them from dirt and sand.

An adult male bearded dragon has a dark "beard," which turns black when he is trying to attract a mate.

The bearded dragon has a pouch on its throat that is covered in spines.

When predators threaten, the lizard escapes fast on its short, strong legs.

In the morning, some bearded dragon lizards **absorb** heat by **basking** in the sun. Although they can look threatening, they are not dangerous to people.

1. The sun has just risen in the sky. A bearded dragon lizard climbs a fence to warm itself in the sun's rays. A little girl sees the lizard leaning on the fence post.

2. She runs across the grass to have a closer look at it. The bearded dragon lizard thinks she is going to attack. It puffs up its body and spreads its spines to make itself look larger than it really is. The little girl runs away in fright.

Size

Did You Know?

Bearded dragons use signals. They wave an arm to say hello to other dragons, move their heads up and down to threaten enemies, and raise their tails to signal danger.

Where in the World

There are seven species of bearded dragon lizard living in Australia in dry deserts, grasslands, forests, **scrubland** and wet coastal areas. Only five of the seven species have "beards."

Glossary

absorb — to take something in
basking — lying down in the sun to gain warmth
bluff — to trick or frighten by pretending to have some power or strength
burrow — an underground home dug by an animal
camouflage — to disguise or hide
chromatophores — skin cells that can change color in many lizards and some other animals
crest — a raised line or ridge of skin on an animal
digest — to break down food in the body
flexible — able to bend easily without breaking
focus — to look at very closely
forked tongue — a tongue split into two parts at the end
glands — parts of the body that make special chemicals needed for the body to work properly
glides — to move through the air without flying
grooves — hollow channels or marks
ground dweller — an animal that lives on the ground
habitats — places where an animal usually lives
highlands — lands high up in the mountains or hills
inhabit — to live in
lizard — one of a large group of reptiles that have long, scaly bodies, four legs, and a pointed tail
mangrove — any evergreen tree or shrub with stiltlike roots that grows thickly along coasts

marsupials — animals that carry their young in pouches, including kangaroos, opossums, and wombats
mongoose — a cat-sized mammal that eats fruit and small animals
nocturnal — active at night
paralyze — to make it impossible to move
predators — animals that hunt other animals for food
prey — an animal hunted for food
reptile — air-breathing creature that usually has a body covered with scaly or bony plates, including alligators, lizards, and snakes
rain forests — thick forests where a lot of rain falls
rival — competing over the same thing
savannas — open grasslands, scattered with bushes and trees
scrublands — lands covered with small shrubs or trees
snout — short, flat nose
territory — land that an animal claims as its own
tree-dwelling — living in trees
tropical — referring to the warmest regions of the world, with lush plant life and lots of rain
venom — a poison made by an animal
webbed — covered in a thin layer of skin

For More Information

Books

Amazing Lizards. Hello Reader (series). Fay Robinson (Cartwheel)

Cool Chameleons. Hello Reader (series). Fay Robinson (Cartwheel)

Illustrated Wildlife Encyclopedia: Reptiles. Barbara Taylor (Lorenz Books)

Keeping Lizards. Unusual Pets (series). David Manning (Barron's Educational Series)

Lizards. Lola M. Schaefer (Heinemann-Raintree)

Lizards, Frogs, and Polliwogs. Douglas Florian (Harcourt Children's Books)

Lizards Weird and Wonderful. Margery Facklam (Little, Brown)

Web Sites

Animal Planet
www.animal.discovery.com/convergence/lizards/lizards.html

CyberSleuthkids
cybersleuth-kids.com/sleuth/Science/Animals/Reptiles/Lizards

Cyclura.com
www.cyclura.com

Green Iguana
www.thewildones.org/Animals/iguana.html

The Texas Horned Lizard
www.whozoo.org/AnlifeSS2001/natdavid/NGD_HornedLizard.htm

Index

Africa 7, 9, 11, 23, 25
Arizona 17, 21
Asia 15, 27
Australia 13, 29

basilisk lizard 4–5
basking
   bearded dragon 29
   Jackson's chameleon 9
   Nile monitor 24
bearded dragon 28–29
burrow 17

California 17
camouflage of
   basilisk lizard 4
   flying lizard 14
   frilled lizard 12
   ground chameleon lizard 6
   Nile monitor 24
Central America 5, 19
chameleons 6–11
chromatophores 10
claws of
   basilisk lizard 4
   gila monster 16
   green iguana 18
   Nile monitor 24
   Salvadori's monitor 26
crest 5
crocodile 25

digesting 20

eggs, Nile monitor 25

feet of
   basilisk lizard 5
   flying lizard 14
   gila monster 16
   leaf-tailed gecko 22
   panther chameleon 10
   webbed 5
fighting 7, 11
flying lizard 14–15
frilled lizard 12–13

geckos 15, 22–23
gila monster 16–17
glands 18
gliding 14
green iguana 18–19
ground chameleon lizard 6–7
ground dweller 6

horns 8, 20
hunting methods
   flying lizard 15
   gila monster 17
   Jackson's chameleon 8, 9

Jackson's chameleon 8–9

leaf-tailed gecko 22–23
legs of
   basilisk lizard 4
   bearded dragon 28
   gila monster 16
   ground chameleon lizard 7
lizard 4

Madagascar 7, 11, 23
mangrove swamps 27
marsupials 15
Mexico 17, 19, 21
monitors 24–27
mouth 10, 12, 13

Nevada 17
New Guinea 13, 27
New Mexico 17, 21
Nile monitor 24–25
North America 17

panther chameleon 10–11
paralyzing 17
pets, green iguana 19
predators and
   ground chameleon lizard 7
   leaf-tailed gecko 23
   regal horned lizard 21
prey of
   flying lizard 15
   gila monster 17
   ground chameleon lizard 6, 7
   Jackson's chameleon 8, 9
   Nile monitor 24, 25
   regal horned lizard 20, 21

regal horned lizard 20–21
reptiles 13
rivalry 7

Salvadori's monitor 26–27
savannas 7

scales
   bearded dragon 28
   frilled lizard 12
   gila monster 16
   green iguana 18
snakes 15, 17, 25
snout 26
South America 5, 19

tail of
   basilisk lizard 4
   flying lizard 14, 15
   gila monster 16
   ground chameleon lizard 6
   leaf-tailed gecko 22
   Nile monitor 24
   panther chameleon 10
   Salvadori's monitor 26
Tanzania 9
territory 7
tongues
   forked 17
   flying lizard 15
   gila monster 17
   ground chameleon lizard 6
   Jackson's chameleon 8, 9
tree-dwelling lizard 6, 14
tropical 7

United States 17, 21
Utah 17

venom 16